Fairy Pathways

Published by Sparrow House Collective
www.sparrowhousecollective.com

ISBN: 978-0-9730616-4-2
Copyright 2020 by Sparrow House Collective

All rights reserved. No part of this book may be reproduced or transmitted in any form or by any means, electronic or mechanical, including photocopying, recording, or by any information storage and retrieval system, without permission, in writing, from the publisher.

Photography by Ellen Hooge
Fairy illustrations by Jordan He

The Temperate Rainforest

Long ago, the Lynn Valley was awe-inspiring. Its trees towered to the clouds and spread root systems deep into the earth, providing food and shelter for thousands of living things.

The forest was logged, stripped of its green riches, and abandoned to mend itself in 1863. Fifty years later, the Lynn Canyon, beautiful once again, caught the eye of developers who donated the land for the park we enjoy today.

Ellen and Jordan dedicate this book to the rare temperate rainforests of our world. This unique habitat is often endangered by logging, urban sprawl, and pollution. We feel privileged to amble through the magical Lynn Canyon rainforest of Vancouver, British Columbia. It is home to bear, deer, coyotes, raccoons, squirrels, birds, mice, salamanders, banana slugs, countless insects, and then there's the fairies we think we saw . . .

One day within a misty wood,
I saw a place where fairies should
be walking up a pathway green,
when visiting the fairy queen.

I thought I heard a tiny sound
but when I stopped and looked around,
I only saw a place where they
had left their footprints on the way.

When wandering by a sparkling brook,
the air beside me gently shook.
I thought I glimpsed a gossamer wing
and heard some silver voices sing.

I found a clearing in the glen,
where fairy dancers now and then
would have a party in the rain,
all glistening with joy again.

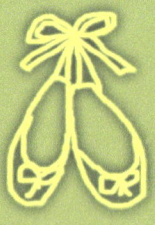

And then I stumbled on a place,
that seemed to banish noise and haste.
So peaceful was the scented air,
I thought I felt them sleeping there.

Around the corner I did spy,
a place to build a castle high.
and thought a fairy knight did ride,
his tiny unicorn, with pride.

A fairy wedding, shining bright,
was celebrated on this site,
where deep within a leafy grove,
the air still lingers thick with love.

And here, a noisy waterfall
covers up a fairy's call,
as all the fairy children dive
into the waters deep and live.

They swing upon the branches high
and meet for kisses in the sky,
then scatter dewdrops on the ground,
but not a trace of them I found.

And so I walked around the bend
in hopes to meet a fairy friend,
and saw a hidden place where they
did share their secrets on the way.

I almost heard their singing sweet,
and almost felt their dancing feet.
I almost saw their tiny wings,
and felt the thrill a forest brings.

Ellen Hooge loves writing, photography, and her grandchildren. She took the photos for this book while on a walk in Lynn Canyon Park, North Vancouver, British Columbia. And, when her granddaughter, Jordan, began pointing out the places along the trail where fairies may have been doing things, the words to *Fairy Pathways* came into being. Ellen lives with her husband, Jack, in Calgary, Alberta. She has written teaching curriculum, magazine articles, and several books. Take a look at some of her projects at: www.sparrowhousecollective.com.

Jordan He lives in Duncan, British Columbia with her mom, dad, two brothers, her cat Skittles, and her dog Mudd. When she was six years old she went on a walk with her grandmother and imagined what the fairies would be doing along the trails of the beautiful rain forest of the Lynn Canyon. Then she went home and drew the fairies she imagined on her walk. She hopes *Fairy Pathways* will inspire children everywhere to enjoy the power of imagination, and to take care of our forests.

www.ingramcontent.com/pod-product-compliance
Lightning Source LLC
Chambersburg PA
CBHW042145290426
44110CB00002B/122